W0007659

No Matter the Time

Fortesa Latifi

WORDS DANCE PUBLISHING

WordsDance.com

Copyright © Fortesa Latifi 2016

No part of this book may be used or performed without written consent from the author except for in critical articles & reviews.

1st Edition
ISBN-13: 978-0-9979404-1-1
ISBN-10: 0-9979404-1-7

Cover photo by Greg Rakozy
Cover design & interior layout by Amanda Oaks

Type set in Bergamo & Malina

Words Dance Publishing
WordsDance.com

to anyone who has ever held
a piece of my wild, chasing heart

No Matter the Time
Fortesa Latifi

"...he consoled himself with the fact that, in the real world, when he looked closely into the darkness he might find the presence of a light, damaged and bruised, but a little light all the same."

— Colum McCann,
Let The Great World Spin

No Matter the Time

From Marilyn Monroe to Arthur Miller

You wanted all of the beauty and none of the truth.
You wanted pearls in the dying afternoon and my hair
falling perfectly down my shoulders. You wanted
martinis during dinner and my body all soft and light
next to yours. You looked at me as though you were
seeing the sun up close and before too long
you learned how a beautiful thing can burn
when you come too near.

It's time to tell the truth now.
Say how gorgeous and lovely
I was from a distance before
you pulled me apart to find
the dead stories inside.
Tell me how you felt more life raft
than human and how you resented
my fingerprints on the inside of your arm.
Tell me what a relief it was when I was gone
and you could remember me how you liked me best—

with my lips painted and my dress ironed, just drunk enough
to be clever and just happy enough to hold your hand
under the table. Forget the truth of it, the great despair
and loss of it. Forget how you loved me until you knew me.
Forget how you never loved me at all.

From Henry Miller to Anais Nin

There is no patience in this body.
There is only enormous wanting.
No one speaks of the stunning weight of it—
how desire pulls us through the world
as though our limbs are attached
to the strings of a clumsy marionette.
I am dizzy with this great burden.
How does one live without love?
At the end of each day, you are there
and this simple act saves me.
I walk through a market to pick peaches
and blush at the thought of your mouth.
All lovers tuck small secrets behind their tongues
and go on clicking through the world
as if they don't know where the light comes from,
as if they didn't create it themselves out of thin air.
I leave the market and walk quickly through the streets.
I open our front door and drop the peaches to the floor.
A week from now, we'll find one rotting under the couch
but for now, there is only enormous wanting.
There is no patience in these bodies.

From Hadley Richardson Hemingway to Ernest Hemingway

I am tugging on our love with both hands
and even that isn't enough to pull you out
of yourself. Darling, you've always had a mind
like a time bomb and I hear it ticking every night.
Thirty years from now it will be splattered across
the foyer of the house you share with your fourth wife
but for now, it is just us and Paris and the lights.
There is a wedding ring on my finger and champagne
every night. We fall asleep to jazz music swimming
in our ears and wake up to strong coffee.
I know things are harder for you than they are for me,
or perhaps anyone, but I just want to be your safe place.
Come rest your crooked heart.
Come rest your tired hands.
Later, you will use them to put a shotgun in your mouth
and follow your father and mine into an early grave
but for now, let me hold them. Let me kiss them.
We're alright,
if only in this moment.

From Coretta Scott King to Martin Luther King Jr.

I loved you knowing the blood would come.
I loved you knowing people in the streets
would be chanting your name. I dreamt
of you before I loved you and woke
holding my hand out for yours.
Nothing has changed, sweetheart.
I always knew there was a war
out there and the best way
to face it has always been
together.

From Frank Butler to Annie Oakley

My girl. My rifle-wielding, boot-wearing,
razor-lipped girl. They didn't expect you
and that made winning all the sweeter.
Every night, a different city. Every night,
the same stage. The train carried us
through the country with your lips
in my ear. Everything was sweet
in those days. Everything was sugar
melting through my fingers.
When you were gone, I couldn't eat
anymore and everyone called it romantic
but it was sharper than that.
It was survival.

From Pierre Curie to Marie Curie

I always dreamed of a partner
who would not walk in front
of me nor behind but beside,
& then you came, with your brilliant
mind and your sore heart bleeding
for three hundred reasons all at the same time.
The world has never seen a person
with more passion. The world has never
seen a person with more purpose.
During the day, there was the lab
and the elements; the experiments
and the hypotheses. During the night,
there was our daughter asleep beside us,
her tiny chest rising and falling; the wood
of our house breathing raggedly as it struggled
to stay upright; our hushed voices dancing in the dark.
For all we could explain with science, how my heart
yearned for yours my whole life slipped through
the slats of reason and it was all the more beautiful for it.

From Franklin Delano Roosevelt to Eleanor Roosevelt

So there was the sickness—my swinging, useless legs;
your mother's throat closing quietly; my father's softly
choking heart. There were the pills and the hot baths
and your hands pressed down on my broken body.
There were the children and how we swam in the pool
in the bright heat of the summer and afterward,
the lemonade full and sugared in the shade.
It wasn't all beautiful and I'm sorry for that.
I'm sorry for the other women and how that left
you in the arms of other lovers and I'm sorry
about the strangled screams pushed into pillows
and I'm sorry about the way love can fail us.
I'm sorry about the way I failed us.
The truth is this: love is something
that must be tended to.
Turn your eyes for a moment
and it drowns
in the very water which once
sustained it.

From Juan Peron to Eva Peron

An entire country, laid at your feet.
An entire country, marching toward your voice.
My love, they only called you a sinner
when they were scared of your clout.
My love, they only called you a saint
when they were scared of your bite.
The truth was hard to swallow
and their mouths were too small.
I'll say it here.

You were never afraid
or if you were, you hid it in the flowers.
If you were, you sat in the sun with your hands
in the dirt and it looked so beautiful
that no one smelled the fear.

From Jack Robinson to Rachel Robinson

Some rocks erode under pressure
and some become diamonds.
You know the pressure I'm speaking of—
how it pushed at the edges of our marriage,
how it stuck its ugly nose against the glass of our home.
How could they have known how protected we were inside?
How committed we were to building a safe haven,
a soft spot in a world gone mad, a quiet place
to lay our heads at the end of another day
spent fighting.
So love was another word for sanctuary.
So family was another word for shelter.
So we fought all day against the limits others set for us
and at night, we sank into each other's arms and smiled
across the dinner table at our children who placed creased napkins
in their laps and bowed their heads in prayer.
Outside, the world continued screaming
but we couldn't hear a thing.

From Alice Toklas to Gertrude Stein

Everyone wanted to breathe the same air as you.
You remember, don't you? How they would flit
in and out of the apartment, drawn to you as moths
toward a flame. You were always the grand one,
the artist, the writer filled with beautiful ideas
that everyone wanted to swallow quickly enough
to feel the warmth like the absinthe that we drank
on the bad days. Oh, the bad days, when the words
wouldn't come, the bad days when the streets filled
with rain and you couldn't fashion a boat out of anything.
I was there all the while. Everyone walked past me
but if they had looked, they would have seen
my eyes always on you.

From Shah Jahan to Mumtaz Mahal

One of the mysteries of the universe
is how something so beautiful—
a child made from our own flesh,
our blood mixing and running through
a new life, our love taking solid form—
could end so horribly.

I can trace the beginning
of your death to us bringing our bodies
together in the fading light of the evening.
We laughed afterwards and you kissed my lips
before falling asleep beside me.
Without our knowledge,
the hourglass tipped.
The beads ran quietly
to the other side
as we slept.

The entire kingdom turned to attention
when they found out you were gone
and even with thousands mourning you,
I was entirely alone with the wild monster of grief.
Look what grief made of me, my love.
The first night without you, I walked through
the rooms where our children slept and touched each
of their faces. I held their small hands
and cradled their growing bodies.
How else was I to be close to you?

Twenty-two years. One thousand elephants.
Twenty thousand men. When we finally
laid your body to rest in that castle,
I wept with relief.

Historians call it a wonder of the world.
They, of course, are speaking of the castle
and I, of course, of our love.

From Richard Loving to Mildred Loving

I will always remember the 90-mile drive
we took that day, to a place where our love
could be called by its proper name.
I think we made it in about an hour
with my foot on the gas pedal and your hand
on my leg. There were a few weeks of bliss after that
where there was always coffee boiling
on the stovetop in the muted cold
of a Virginia morning and you reading
in bed next to me at night. Who could've
called that a crime scene? Who could've
called that anything other than a miracle?
We found out when the police broke down
the door while we were sleeping.
We found out when we were kept in separate jail cells,
our child growing quietly inside of you.
We found out when they made us leave home and never look back
but baby, we looked back. We looked back and we fought
like hell and five years later, we laughed and cried
when the gavel came down in our favor.
Finally the world knew.
What they saw as sin
was really salvation all along.

From Virginia Woolf to Leonard Woolf

Picture this:
my heart as a fist, unfurling its fingers;
as a typewriter, clumsily sliding to the left to begin again;
as a new book, cracked open and breathing into the sunlight.

Picture this:
a womb quiet and empty year after year;
a body haunted and screaming;
a husband with his head in hands at the side of a hospital bed.

Picture this:
a river, delicious and beckoning;
a woman, white flag clutched between her fingers;
a pile of stones, heavy and forgiving.

My love. My sweet love.
I am sorry but you must understand.
I wanted to free you.
I filled my pockets and I freed you.

From Simone de Beauvoir to Jean-Paul Sartre

Forget the ring and the dress and the kitchen tiles needing
to be scrubbed. Forget the white veil and the crowd holding glasses
of champagne and dinner needing to be made.
I wanted to move beyond all of that and there you were,
with me the whole while. We didn't need the wedding
or the roses or the church—hell, we built our own cathedral
out of thought and intelligence and gin. I loved your brain
as much as I've ever loved anything and that was enough
to see us through. Freedom was as important to us as love
and after we'd had enough of the freedom, we could always find
each other. That was the important part—
we always had each other.

From Jane Hawking to Stephen Hawking

This is the beauty of youth:
even illness seems small
when viewed through
the radiant prism
the young hold
in their smooth hands.
You were sick but I loved you.
You were dying but I loved you.

When I stood in front of our families
in a white dress, you were already leaning
on a cane. Later, our first child learned to walk
when for you, there was only the unlearning.
For all your talk of time, we never spoke
of how cruel it could be—how time dragged you
backwards, until you couldn't walk; how it yanked
you forward, until you couldn't speak; how it aged you
and tormented me and tired us both.

Looking back, I would tell my younger self only this:
even the surest love can be ripped to pieces in the face
of such grand degeneration.
Even the people who are supposed to help
will be the ones sharpening the knives.
Even you will learn how to use them.
Some days you will love him less
but every day you will love him.
It won't last forever, not in the way
you imagined on your wedding day,
but in another way, it will never end.
There will be other white dresses
and other rings adorning your finger.
With this, there will be a brilliant ache.
With this, there will be an incredible relief.

On our first date, you told me of how stars collapse
in on themselves in the face of black holes.
To this day, I can't figure out which one of us
did the collapsing and which one us did the swallowing.
All I know is that in the moment in between,
there was such blinding light.

What was it that you told me once, Stephen?
That nothing ever dies in the universe—
it is only reborn as something else.

From Mark Antony to Cleopatra

My god, the crooked path.
My god, the bodies lying
across it. My god, your belly
swelling in the candlelight.
My god, our children with
your mouth and my eyes.
My god, the world at war
and us at the center of it all.
My god, the beauty of love
in the middle of war.
My god, the ending.
My god, the blood.
My god, the last breath.
My god, the sweet relief.

From Jacqueline Kennedy Onassis to John Fitzgerald Kennedy

There was so much loss in our love. I suppose that's the way
the world turns. For every beautiful thing, there is one horrible.
In that case, I hate the world. I hate the world for what it gave to me
and what it took away. First were the babies—the babies, Jack,
our babies. I will never be able to measure the grief of holding
our sweet children in my body for nine months and losing them
afterwards. I know I was lost too during those days
and I hope you'll forgive me but the death of a child
is like being awake inside of a nightmare.
Even afterwards, with Caroline and John, I cherished every scream
and every tear as though each were to show how alive they were.
After the babies, I lost you, Jack, and I swear I thought
that would be the end of my life. You looked so handsome
that day in your suit and tie. It seems impossible
that a terrible thing could happen on such a beautiful day,
with the sun shining through your skull
as it was ripped apart. I carried a piece of it
into the emergency room even after it was clear
there would be no use for it.
I couldn't let go of any piece of you, Jack.
You understand, don't you?
I never could let go.

From June Carter Cash to Johnny Cash

I tell you I love you then take it back,
pulling on the edges of it like so many miles
of fishing reel. At the end of it, something is gutted.
At the end of it, something is split open and screaming.
A chalky white pill is in each of our mouths and if this isn't love,
then we're totally fucked. If this isn't love, then we lost the map.
Imagine a place where nothing bad had to happen
to make us good people. Imagine a place where
we first met during the day, in the sunlight,
on the green, green grass. That place doesn't exist of course,
but it's nice to think about. Just don't pin your hopes to it.
Just remember to open the window.
Otherwise, you're stuck.
Otherwise, you won't remember
all the other easier places to breathe.

From Amelia Earhart to George Putnam

I already loved so many things by the time
I came to love you and you, darling man,
you knew this and understood it well.
I showed you the space I had for you
and you nodded, as if to say *that will do*
and it did.

I will always love you
for taking that space without demanding more.
I will always love you
for making that space feel like home.

From Richard Burton to Elizabeth Taylor

The very first moment I met you, you stilled my shaking hands
and wrapped them around a cup of coffee, lifting it to my lips,
and I drank and was warm and evened out, just like that.
One day, your hands would shake with mine and we wouldn't
have anywhere to turn to be still but we didn't know that then.
So our love was the vodka, cold in a martini glass kissing an olive,
setting us trembling. So our love was the coffee, warm in a mug
mixing with a drop of milk, setting us straight. The whole world
watched you and knew you were beautiful and damn if I wasn't
the luckiest man alive to know it up close. I only wish we could
have done a better job with it. I wanted a different ending.
I wanted a better story.
I wanted you there all along.

From Oscar Wilde to Alfred Douglas

Well, every lover tells the other they'll give the world for them—
oh, that gleaming promise, dancing in the candlelight—
but how many are held to it? Wasn't I held, my dear boy?
By the jury and the judge and the restless rusting shackles?

The worst of it wasn't the ruin or the decay or the days wasted
behind the iron bars of a cell. The worst of it was the prosecutor
holding our love up to the light and calling it dirty. The worst of it
was the alphabet of our devotion passed
in front of eyes which
could not hope to read it.

What they didn't know
was the cage was unnecessary.
What they didn't know was that prison
was anywhere you weren't.

The moral of the story is this:
in a thousand lifetimes,
in a thousand ways,
I would give the world for you.
Haven't I already?

From Jane Addams to Mary Rozet Smith

When I had to walk through the world
without you—even for a moment,
even for a day—I carried a canvas
smeared with the colors of your face
and your mouth and your holy, holy hips.
In this way, love is not graceful.
Who among us would choose to carry such a thing?
On trains, I spoke under my breath to passerby—
pardon me, pardon me, I know this package is in the way.
On buses, I fell asleep holding you to my chest
and woke with indentations pressed into my face.
In this way, love is clumsy.
I know there was a time when I existed without you
but that time has come and gone and I'm standing
on the other side of it now, missing you like hell.
In this way, love is grand.
I only want to be home with you.
I am on my way. There is only one more train ride.
I'll see you soon.

From Allen Ginsberg to Peter Orlovsky

The poet sees a bruise and compares it to their lover's lips.
The poet presses their fingers into the blue heart of it and laughs
between mouthfuls of aspirin. The poet cringes at the idea
of a closed door but stays firmly on the other side of it.
The poet is not ashamed because shame would be too easy.
The poet throws a blown glass pipe across the room just to see
it shatter. The poet thinks destruction is simple.
Picking up the broom and apologizing
to the glass is what's hard.
Some days, I am the glass.
Some days, you are.
Either way, we shatter.

From Azem Galica to Shote Galica

I didn't want the fight. I didn't want the war
or the blood rusting in a puddle on the floor.
I didn't want the shovels or the dirt thrown
over my shoulder in the name of defeat
but when you love something enough,
you put on the uniform. You clean your gun.
That's what the politicians don't understand—
even war is about love. Even love is about country.
We are all fighting for the smallest of moments—
to go home and drink strong tea in our own kitchens;
to kiss our children's faces just as they are rising from sleep;
to eat with our hands with three generations of family unfolded
in the same room. In the middle of a summer afternoon,
these dreams are lost, the flame of a candle blown out
by death's breath. Darling, who but you could have faced death
with such grace? Who but you could have faced war
with such resolve? So I'm gone now.
This is the human price of war.
We always knew this, but now it is close.
This time, you are kneeling over my grave.
There is no miracle here. Every life on earth
ends in this spot. The miraculous part is you
putting on your uniform and cleaning your gun.
The miraculous part is you shouldering grief
and pulling it through the mountains with you.
The miraculous part is your muscles stretching
and growing underneath it. The miraculous part
is how you never stopped fighting, even for a second.

From Anne Boleyn to Henry VIII

Everyone wants to be a martyr for love.
The whole world over, people think it is the grandest
possibility for a life: to live for love
and to die for it. It's not as clean as that.
One moment, there are lips on my neck
and the next, there is a sword.
Tell me how to make sense of this.
Tell me how love is turned on its head,
how it grows spoiled and dirty in the afternoon light.
How a promise is meant in the moment it is uttered
but holds no life beyond that.
I only wish to say this:
dying for love is still death.
There is no beauty to be found here.

From Ava Gardner to Frank Sinatra

I don't think we could've done a better job
with it, baby. I think we gave it all we had.
I think there was so much love between us
that we went mad with it. We spun through
the world on a golden thread, laughing all the while.
My lost love. My beautiful boy. Tell me you remember
those first nights—how they stretched on forever towards morning,
how we laughed in the dying light and made more coffee,
how we swore at the clocks and demanded they make more time for us,
that they give us just a moment to sit in the light of what we'd found.
Time doesn't stop, as it turns out. How many lovers before us
realized this exact thing and screamed at the knowledge of it?
Those first nights, we did our damn best.
Those first nights, we locked the doors
and invented a newer, better love for ourselves,
one that wouldn't fail or falter or be left to die.
Remember how sure we were? Remember how young?
Those were the most beautiful times.
Don't talk about what came after—
the knife held to the wrist and the gin bottles
empty and glistening and the nights we spent
on different sides of the world destroying ourselves
because we didn't know how to live in a world
where this love couldn't be salvaged.
I don't want to think of that.
I want to think of your lips tracing my ribs
and your breath hot at my throat.
I want to remember that new, aching time
when we carved out space in our bodies for each other.
Don't talk about the emptiness now.
Just remember how full it was.
Just remember how beautiful.
I only want to remember how we loved each other
before we learned that love wasn't enough.

From Elizabeth Hamilton to Alexander Hamilton

I wanted a smaller life once I met you.
They say love unfurls the world like a once-folded map
but for me, everything narrowed. I only wanted you.
In my dreams, we built a house at the end of a street
lined with sycamore trees and there was never a reason
to cry. The shutters were blue and the trim was white.
The children were happy and they buried us in the end.
The truth of it was nothing like this. We existed on a grand scale.
Everything was beautiful and cracked, like most great things.
Of all the letters we wrote back and forth,
this is the only thing left.
You can understand that, can't you?
Everything was already destroyed.
All I did was light the match.

From Kurt Cobain to Courtney Love

The pills and the ashtrays and the needles
pushing into your milk white skin.
The curtains pulled tight around the windows and
flowers rotting slowly in a cracked vase
and your fingers wrapped around my shaking wrist.
Crushed cocaine melting between our tongues
and your hips sleeping between the sheets
and our guitars leaning against each other
in the corner of the room. It was beautiful
in the way that broken things are beautiful.
It was love in the way that two people with their
hands closed around each other's throats is love.
Which is to say, of course it was.
A body isn't any less of a body for the bruises.

From Zelda Sayre Fitzgerald to F. Scott Fitzgerald

We're completely mad together but we call it love and that's
what matters. Remember when we first met and you threw
me a birthday party? My father frowned and made me leave
early. I didn't even get to taste the cocktail you named after
me. We were so young then. We didn't know anything of love
but we decided to figure it out together
and that's what counts.
Forget about what came later. I don't want to talk
about the fights and the plates thrown across the kitchen
of our first apartment and the things we said and then took back
but could never actually take back. We're at the end now
and I'll remember it how I like. I'll remember my hair swept
across my face during our first dance and you, so handsome
in your uniform. You never did make it to the war but you
had plenty of your own. And I loved you through them all.
I don't think I ever had any other choice.

About the Author

Fortesa Latifi is a 23-year old poet who calls the desert home. She is a student at the Walter Cronkite School of Journalism at Arizona State University pursuing a Masters degree in Journalism and Mass Communication. This is her third collection of poetry. Her work has been published through *To Write Love On Her Arms*, *Kosovo 2.0*, and *Vagabond City Lit*. She is so glad you are holding this in your hands.

Acknowledgments

R & D-
for being the first love story I ever knew.

Z & A-
for making me smile on the most impossible of days.

A-
for this love.

L, N, & T-
for being such beautiful friends.

Amanda & Words Dance-
for believing in this idea.

& you-
for reading.

WORDS DANCE PUBLISHING has one aim:

　　　To spread mind-blowing / heart-opening poetry.

Words Dance artfully & carefully wrangles words that were born to dance wildly in the heart-mind matrix. Rich, edgy, raw, emotionally-charged energy balled up & waiting to whip your eyes wild; we rally together words that were written to make your heart go boom right before they slay your mind.

Words Dance Publishing is an independent press out of Pennsylvania. We work closely & collaboratively with all of our writers to ensure that their words continue to breathe in a sound & stunning home. Most importantly though, we leave the windows in these homes unlocked so you, the reader, can crawl in & throw one fuck of a house party.

To learn more about our books, authors, events & Words Dance Poetry Magazine, visit:

WORDSDANCE.COM

Other titles available from
WORDS DANCE PUBLISHING

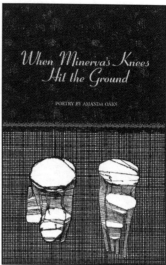

FREE PDF EBOOKS

WHERE'D YOU PUT THE KEYS GIRL + WHEN MINERVA'S KNEES HIT THE GROUND
Poetry by Amanda Oaks

DOWNLOAD HERE:

http://wordsdance.com/free-stuff

Music-inspired digital chapbooks by *Words Dance* Founder, Amanda Oaks. These collections were made with deep love & respect for Tori Amos' + Deftones' music & are made up of erasure poems created from select songs from each artist's catalog + each of the erasure poems are paired an original sister poem & the title of that sister poem is a short lyric from the songs chosen.

"Oaks' original poems, which accompany the erasures, are among the best of her work to date. They are urgent and striking. This is the work of a fully confident poet hitting her stride."

— KENDALL A. BELL
Publisher/Editor @ *Maverick Duck Press*

Crybaby by Caitlyn Siehl

The Goddess Songs by Azra Tabassum

Why I'm Not Where You Are by Brianna Albers

Before the First Kiss by Ashe Vernon & Trista Mateer

Our Bodies & Other Fine Machines by Natalie Wee

holyFool by Amanda Oaks

Other titles available from
WORDS DANCE PUBLISHING

A FIELD OF BLOOMING BRUISES
Poetry by Schuyler Peck

| $12 | 58 pages | 5.5" x 8.5" | softcover |

ISBN: 978-0692628591

To my first year of recovery, my first impression was wrong, you turned out much sweeter than I thought. To my followers, who inspire me daily with their kindness; for all the friends I haven't met yet. To my friends, you are every light I've ever looked for. To my Tyler, for giving me enough love, I can fill books with it.

"Peck's poems carry both a lovely fragility and a sense of strength, and it is a testament to her prowess as a poet that she comes out of her trials all that much stronger because of it. While some poems here are stronger than others, nothing here is boring or ordinary. There is a warmth to Peck's words, and she wears her soft nature with no sense of shame. You could lump her in with similar poets like Clementine Von Radics and Charlotte Erikkson, but she's better than both of them, and has the potential to be one of the best contemporary poets, in time."

— **KENDALL A. BELL**
Publisher/Editor @ *Maverick Duck Press*

Other titles available from
WORDS DANCE PUBLISHING

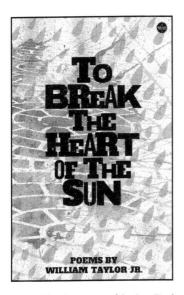

TO BREAK THE HEART OF THE SUN

Poetry by William Taylor Jr.

| $15 | 132 pages | 5.5" x 8.5" | softcover |

ISBN: 978-0692617380

"*In To Break the Heart of the Sun* Taylor invites you over for a few drinks & then takes you out on the gritty streets of San Francisco. You dip into the bars & cafés in the Tenderloin & North Beach, you skirt the sidewalks down Haight, in Chinatown & the Mission, all the while bonding over the people you love, music, poetry, past loves, friendship, your childhoods & dreams. You question life, both the dark & light of it, looking for the truth of it. You laugh & weep with the people you meet along the way, every face some kind of prayer. Taylor teaches you how to dance with your joy while dressed in your sorrow. He has a way of showing you how keep your heart open & closed at the same time so you don't lose your footing, but if you do, with kind eyes & laughter escaping both your lips, his hand reaches down to help you up."

"William Taylor, Jr, my pick for best poet in San Francisco, is back with *To Break the Heart of the Sun*, and it's every bit a Taylor book, every bit as sad, and beautiful, and even begrudgingly hopeful as all his best work. Or, if not hopeful, that at least graceful in its wise and simple acceptance of the silly problem called life. His lines crackle and sing, sweeping through the crumbling landscape of the Tenderloin, and the vast, Buddha-like landscape of his inner life. These poems will save something otherwise lost even as we fumbling, stuttering mortals fade...and I can think of no higher honor than that. And Amanda at Words Dance has put together a drop-dead gorgeous book, with cover-art on par with those sublime Black Sparrow covers of years past...so there is absolutely nothing but praise for this entire glorious project. Treat yourself to a copy!"

— **HOSHO MCCREESH**
Author of *A Deep and Gorgeous Thirst*

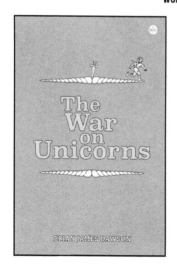

THE WAR ON UNICORNS
Poetry by Brian James Dawson

| $12 | 74 pages | 5.5" x 8.5" | softcover |

ISBN: 978-0692487754

"*The War on Unicorns*, with its parts 1 through 40, which from its opening lines- *The dog barks constantly. Shining men in / riot gear accept flowers.* – enters the conflicting imaginations of the local and the empyreal. The book itself is a halcyonian triumph. Lines, of course, abound. *A paper airplane flies towards a furnace* (2). *A remade red dress / hangs lugubriously on a wooden rack / in a closet left over from / the Mormon migration* (5). But I've said too much of what it merely says. It doesn't build, it contains, it is house. Inside, there is map enough to distract the bombings. At one point, Dawson directs us to *Remember Tehran*. It is not jarring, it is just the end of a poem. Dawson is a student of history but teaches the sane myth."

— **BARTON SMOCK**

Author of *Misreckon* & *The Blood You Don't See Is Fake*

"The poems in *The War on Unicorns* are perfect examples of the best words in the best order. I love the snap-shot feel of each poem, and if a picture is worth a thousand words, then these word-pictures are golden. *Piles/of old newspapers /yellow in the long light/of a sequester sun* and *he wishes-wishes to retract all his lies / and rake them into multi-colored piles.* The observation of human experiences and relationships are sharp - *I am the curator of the universe's / museum of cruel jokes.* This writing has both style and substance. *Take off your armor; unlock your heart* - you should buy this book."

— **VIOLET WILD**

Other titles available from
WORDS DANCE PUBLISHING

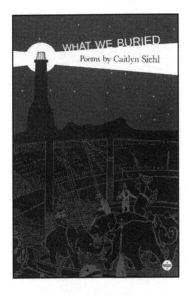

WHAT WE BURIED
Poetry by Caitlyn Siehl

| $12 | 64 pages | 5.5" x 8.5" | softcover |

ISBN: 978-0615985862

GOODREADS CHOICE AWARD NOMINEE FOR POETRY (2014)

This book is a cemetery of truths buried alive. The light draws you in where you will find Caitlyn there digging. When you get close enough, she'll lean in & whisper, Baby, buried things will surface no matter what, get to them before they get to you first. Her unbounded love will propel you to pick up a shovel & help— even though the only thing you want to do is kiss her lips, kiss her hands, kiss every one of her stretch marks & the fire that is raging in pit of her stomach. She'll see your eyes made of devour & sadness, she'll hug you & say, Baby, if you eat me alive, I will cut my way out of your stomach. Don't let this be your funeral. Teach yourself to navigate the wound.

"It takes a true poet to write of love and desire in a way that manages to surprise and excite. Caitlyn Siehl does this in poem after poem and makes it seem effortless. Her work shines with a richness of language and basks in images that continue to delight and astound with multiple readings. *What We Buried* is a treasure from cover to cover."

— **WILLIAM TAYLOR JR.**
Author of *An Age of Monsters*

Other titles available from
WORDS DANCE PUBLISHING

BELLY OF THE BEAST
Poetry by Ashe Vernon

| $12 | 82 pages | 5.5" x 8.5" | softcover |

ISBN: 978-0692300541

"Into the *Belly of the Beast* we crawl with Ashe as our guide; into the dark visceral spaces where love, lust, descent and desire work their transformative magic and we find ourselves utterly altered in the reading. A truly gifted poet and truth-spiller, Ashe's metaphors create images within images, leading us to question the subjective truths, both shared and hidden, in personal relationship – to the other, and to oneself. Unflinching in her approach, her poetry gives voice to that which most struggle to admit – even if only to themselves. And as such, *Belly of the Beast* is a work of startling courage and rich depth – a darkly delicious pleasure."

— AMY PALKO
Goddess Guide, Digital Priestess & Writer

"It isn't often you find a book of poetry that is as unapologetic, as violent, as moving as this one. Ashe's writing is intense and visceral. You feel the punch in your gut while you're reading, but you don't question it. You know why it's there and you almost welcome it."

— CAITLYN SIEHL
Author of What We Buried

"The poems you are about to encounter are the fierce time capsules of girl-hood, girded with sharp elbows, surprise kisses, the meanders of wander-lust. We need voices this strong, this true for the singing reminds us that we are not alone, that someone, somewhere is listening for the faint pulse that is our wish to be seen. Grab hold, this voice will be with us forever."

— RA WASHINGTON
GuidetoKulchurCleveland.com

Other titles available from
WORDS DANCE PUBLISHING

DOWRY MEAT
Poetry by Heather Knox

| \$12 | 110 pages | 5.5" x 8.5" | softcover |

ISBN: 978-0692398494

Heather Knox's *Dowry Meat* is a gorgeous, tough-as-nails debut that arrives on your doorstep hungry and full of dark news. There's damage here, and obsession, and more haunted beauty in the wreckage of just about everything—relationships, apartment clutter, rough sex, the body, and of course the just-post apocalypse—than you or I could hope to find on our own. These are poems that remind us not that life is hard—that's old news—but that down there in the gravel and broken glass is where the truth-worth-hearing lies, and maybe the life worth living. If you were a city, Knox tells us, unflinching as always, *I'd… read your graffiti. Drink your tap water./Feel your smog and dirt stick to my sweat… If you were a city, I'd expect to be robbed.*

— **JON LOOMIS**
Author of *Vanitas Motel (winner of the FIELD prize)* and *The Pleasure Principle*

"Heather Knox's debut collection is a lyric wreath made of purulent ribbon and the most inviting of thorns. Tansy and tokophobia, lachrymosity and lavage are braided together in this double collection, which marries a sci-fi Western narrative to a lyric sequence. Both elapse in an impossible location made of opposites—futuristic nostalgia, or erotic displeasure—otherwise known as the universe in which we (attempt to) live."

— **JOYELLE MCSWEENEY**
Author of *The Necropastoral: Poetry, Media, Occults & Salamandrine: 8 Gothics*

"*Dowry Meat*'s apocalyptic fever dream myth-making bleeds into what we might call the poetry of witness or the tradition of the confessional, except that these lines throb with lived experience and a body isn't necessarily a confession. Heather Knox's poems are beautifully wrought and beautifully raw."

— **DORA MALECH**
Author of *Shore Ordered Ocean* & *Say So*

Other titles available from
WORDS DANCE PUBLISHING

THE NO YOU NEVER LISTENED TO
Poetry by Meggie Royer

| \$14 | 142 pages | 5.5" x 8.5" | softcover |

ISBN: 978-0692463635

"It's a strange thing when the highest praise you can offer for someone's work is, "I wish this didn't exist," but that was the refrain that echoed in my head after I read Meggie Royer's third book.

As fans of her work know, Meggie takes the universal and makes it personal. With *The No You Never Listened To*, she takes the personal and makes it universal. As a sexual assault survivor, Meggie is well-acquainted with trauma: the aftermath, the guilt, the anger. She has never shied away from taking Hemingway's advice – write hard and clear about what hurts – and that strength has never been more of an asset than with this body of work.

The No You Never Listened To is the book you will wish you'd had when trauma climbed into your bed. It is the book you will give to friends who are dragged from their "before" into a dark and terrifying "after". And yes, it is the book you will wish didn't exist.

But it is also the one that will remind you, in your darkest moments, where the blame really belongs. It will remind you that your memory will not always be an enemy. And it will remind you that none of us have ever been alone in this."

— CLAIRE BIGGS
To Write Love on Her Arms Editor / Writer

"Nietzsche once warned us to be careful gazing into the abyss, that we run the risk of staring so long that the void consumes us. The poems in this book were born of the abyss, of conflict & trauma & survival. And through these poems, Meggie Royer stares – hard, unflinching, courageous – and instead of gazing back, the abyss looks away."

— WILLIAM JAMES
Drunk In A Midnight Choir editor & author of *rebel hearts & restless ghosts*

Other titles available from
WORDS DANCE PUBLISHING

CHLOE
Poetry by Kristina Haynes

| $12 | 110 pages | 5.5" x 8.5" | softcover |

ISBN: 978-0692386637

Chloe is brave and raw, adolescence mixed with salt. These poems are about how hungry we've been, how foolish, how lonely. Chloe is not quite girl nor woman, full of awkward bravery. Kristina is an electric voice that pulls Chloe apart page after page, her heartbreaks, her too many drinks, her romantic experiences of pleasure and pain. Chloe and Kristina make a perfect team to form an anthem for girls everywhere, an anthem that reassures us we deserve to take up space. Indeed, when I met Chloe, I too thought "This is the closest I've been to anybody in months."

— **MEGGIE ROYER**
Author of *Survival Songs*
and *Healing Old Wounds with New Stitches*

"*Chloe* is one of the most intimate books you'll read all year. Chloe is my new best friend. I want to eat burnt popcorn on her couch and watch Friends reruns. I want to borrow her clothing, write on her walls in lipstick. Chloe is not your dream girl. She doesn't have everything figured out. She's messy. She's always late. She promises old lovers she'll never call again. She teaches you what the word "indulgence" means. She's wonderful, wonderful, wonderful. In *Chloe*, Kristina Haynes digs into the grittiness of modern womanhood, of mothers and confusion and iPhones and two, maybe three-night-stands. Her truths are caramels on the tongue but are blunter, harsher on the way down. Kristina introduces us to a character I'll be thinking about for a very long time. Go read this book. Then write a poem. Then kiss someone. Then buy an expensive strain of tea and a new pillow. Then go read it again."

— **YASMIN BELKHYR**
Editor-in-Chief at *Winter Tangerine Review*

Other titles available from
WORDS DANCE PUBLISHING

LITERARY SEXTS
VOLUME 2

A Collection of Short & Sexy Love Poems

| $12 | 76 pages | 5.5" x 8.5" | softcover |

ISBN: 978-0692359594

This is the highly anticipated second volume of Literary Sexts! After over 1,000 copies of Literary Sexts Volume 1 being sold, we are super-excited to bring you a second volume! Literary Sexts is an annual modern day anthology of short love & sexy poems edited by Amanda Oaks & Caitlyn Siehl. These are poems that you would text to your lover. Poems that you would slip into a back pocket, suitcase, wallet or purse on the sly. Poems that you would write on slips of paper & stick under your crush's windshield wiper or pillow. Poems that you would write on a Post-it note & leave on the bathroom mirror. Poems that you would whisper into your lover's ear. Hovering around 40 contributors & 130 poems, this book reads is like one long & very intense conversation between two lovers. It's absolutely breathtaking.

This is for the leather
& the lace of you—

your flushed cheeks
& what set them ablaze.

Other titles available from
WORDS DANCE PUBLISHING

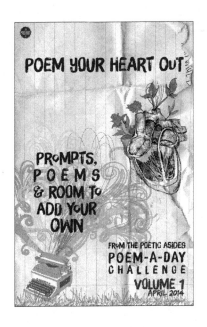

POEM YOUR HEART OUT
Prompts, Poems & Room to Add Your Own
Volume 1

| $15 | 158 pages | 5.5" x 8.5" | softcover |

ISBN: 978-0692317464

PROMPT BOOK • ANTHOLOGY • WORKBOOK

Words Dance Publishing teamed up with the Writer's Digest's Poetic Asides blog to make their Poem-A-Day challenge this year even more spectacular!

Part poetry prompt book, part anthology of the best poems written during the 2014 April PAD (Poem-A-Day) Challenge on the Poetic Asides blog (by way of Writer's Digest) & part workbook, let both, the prompt & poem, inspire you to create your own poetic masterpieces. Maybe you participated in April & want to document your efforts during the month. Maybe you're starting now, like so many before you, with just a prompt, an example poem, & an invitation to poem your heart out! You're encouraged—heck, dared—to write your own poems inside of this book!

This book is sectioned off by Days, each section will hold the prompt for that day, the winning poem for that day & space for you to place the poem you wrote for that day's prompt inside.

Just a few of the guest judges: Amy King, Bob Hicok, Jericho Brown, Nate Pritts, Kristina Marie Darling & Nin Andrews...

Challenge yourself, your friend, a writing workshop or your class to this 30 Day Poem-A-Day Challenge!

THIS IS AN INVITATION To POEM YOUR HEART OUT!

Other titles available from
WORDS DANCE PUBLISHING

I EAT CROW + BLUE COLLAR AT BEST
Poetry by Amanda Oaks + Zach Fishel

| \$15 | 124 pages | 5.5" x 8.5" | softcover |

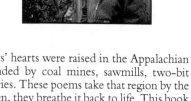

Home is where the heart is and both poets' hearts were raised in the Appalachian region of Western Pennsylvania surrounded by coal mines, sawmills, two-bit hotel taverns, farms, churches and cemeteries. These poems take that region by the throat and shake it until it's bloody and then, they breathe it back to life. This book is where you go when you're looking for nostalgia to kick you in the teeth. This is where you go when you're 200 miles away from a town you thought you'd never want to return to but suddenly you're pining for it.

Amanda and Zach grew up 30 miles from each other and met as adults through poetry. Explore both the male and female perspective of what it's like to grow up hemmed in by an area's economic struggle. These poems mine through life, love, longing and death, they're for home and away, and the inner strength that is not deterred by any of those things.

SPLIT BOOK #1

What are Split Books?

Two full-length books from two poets in one + there's a collaborative split between the poets in the middle!

COLLECT THEM ALL!

Other titles available from
WORDS DANCE PUBLISHING

SHAKING THE TREES
Poetry by Azra Tabassum

| $12 | 72 pages | 5.5" x 8.5" | softcover |

ISBN: 978-0692232408

From the very first page *Shaking the Trees* meets you at the edge of the forest, extends a limb & seduces you into taking a walk through the dark & light of connection. Suddenly, like a gunshot in the very-near distance, you find yourself traipsing though a full-blown love story that you can't find your way out of because the story is actually the landscape underneath your feet. It's okay though, you won't get lost– you won't go hungry. Azra shakes every tree along the way so their fruit blankets the ground before you. She picks up pieces & hands them to you but not before she shows you how she can love you so gently it will feel like she's unpeeling you carefully from yourself. She tells you that it isn't about the bite but the warm juice that slips from the lips down chin. She holds your hand when you're trudging through the messier parts, shoes getting stuck in the muck of it all, but you'll keep going with the pulp of the fruit still stuck in-between your teeth, the juice will dry in the crooks of your elbows & in the lines on your palms. You'll taste bittersweet for days.

"I honestly haven't read a collection like this before, or at least I can't remember having read one. My heart was wrecked by Azra. It's like that opening line in Fahrenheit 451 when Bradbury says, "It was a pleasure to burn." It really was a pleasure being wrecked by it."

— NOURA
of NouraReads

"I wanted to cry and cheer and fuck. I wanted to take the next person I saw and kiss them straight on the lips and say, "Remember this moment for the rest of your life.""

— CHELSEA MILLER

Other titles available from
WORDS DANCE PUBLISHING

POEMS THAT INTEND TO BE SEEN

By Melissa May

SPARKLEFAT
Poetry by Melissa May

| $12 | 62 pages | 5.5" x 8.5" | softcover |

SparkleFat is a loud, unapologetic, intentional book of poetry about my body, about your body, about fat bodies and how they move through the world in every bit of their flash and spark and burst. Some of the poems are painful, some are raucous celebrations, some are reminders and love letters and quiet gifts back to the vessel that has traveled me so gracefully - some are a hymnal of yes, but all of them sparkle. All of them don't mind if you look – really. They built their own house of intention, and they draped that shit in lime green sequins. All of them intend to be seen. All of them have no more fucks to give about a world that wants them to be quiet.

"I didn't know how much I needed this book until I found myself, three pages in, ugly crying on the plane next to a concerned looking business man. This book is the most glorious, glittery pink permission slip. It made me want to go on a scavenger hunt for every speck of shame in my body and sing hot, sweaty R&B songs to it. There is no voice more authentic, generous and resounding than Melissa May. From her writing, to her performance, to her role in the community she delivers fierce integrity & staggering passion. From the first time I watched her nervously step to the mic, to the last time she crushed me in a slam, it is has been an honor to watch her astound the poetry slam world and inspire us all to be not just better writers but better people. We need her."

— **LAUREN ZUNIGA**
Author of *The Smell of Good Mud*

"*SparkleFat* is a firework display of un-shame. Melissa May's work celebrates all of the things we have been so long told deserved no streamers. This collection invites every fat body out to the dance and steams up the windows in the backseat of the car afterwards by kissing the spots we thought (or even hoped) no one noticed but are deserving of love just the same as our mouths."

— **RACHEL WILEY**
Author of *Fat Girl Finishing School*

Other titles available from
WORDS DANCE PUBLISHING

LOVE AND OTHER SMALL WARS

Poetry by Donna-Marie Riley

| $12 | 76 pages | 5.5" x 8.5" | softcover |

ISBN: 978-0615931111

Love and Other Small Wars reminds us that when you come back from combat usually the most fatal of wounds are not visible. Riley's debut collection is an arsenal of deeply personal poems that embody an intensity that is truly impressive yet their hands are tender. She enlists you. She gives you camouflage & a pair of boots so you can stay the course through the minefield of her heart. You will track the lovely flow of her soft yet fierce voice through a jungle of powerful imagery on womanhood, relationships, family, grief, sexuality & love, amidst other matters. Battles with the heart aren't easily won but Riley hits every mark. You'll be relieved that you're on the same side. Much like war, you'll come back from this book changed.

"Riley's work is wise, intense, affecting, and uniquely crafted. This collection illuminates her ability to write with both a gentle hand and a bold spirit. She inspires her readers and creates an indelible need inside of them to consume more of her exceptional poetry. I could read *Love and Other Small Wars* all day long…and I did."

— **APRIL MICHELLE BRATTEN**
editor of *Up the Staircase Quarterly*

"Riley's poems are personal, lyrical and so vibrant they practically leap off the page, which also makes them terrifying at times. A beautiful debut."

— **BIANCA STEWART**

Other titles available from
WORDS DANCE PUBLISHING

LITERARY SEXTS

A Collection of Short & Sexy Love Poems
(Volume 1)

| $12 | 42 pages | 5.5" x 8.5" | softcover |

ISBN: 978-0615959726

Literary Sexts is a modern day anthology of short love poems with subtle erotic undertones edited by Amanda Oaks & Caitlyn Siehl. Hovering around 50 contributors & 124 poems, this book reads is like one long & very intense conversation between two lovers. It's absolutely breathtaking. These are poems that you would text to your lover. Poems that you would slip into a back pocket, suitcase, wallet or purse on the sly. Poems that you would write on slips of paper & stick under your crush's windshield wiper. Poems that you would write on a Post-it note & leave on the bathroom mirror.

HIT #1
ON AMAZON'S
HOT NEW
RELEASE LIST!

"It's like 100+ new ways to make a reader blush. The imagery is so subtle yet completely thrilling..."
NOW I NEED A COLD SHOWER!"
            - K. W.

"**I DEVOURED IT!** I physically wanted to eat these poems. I wanted to wear them on my skin like perfume..."
            - A. G.

"I have consumed this in ways that have left my insides looking like strips of velvet fabric... **SO ORGASMIC!"**
            - K. B.

"**A MAELSTROM OF EMOTIONS!** I only hope that there is a Volume 2, a Volume 3 and so on because I need more of this!"
            - Daniel CZ

Other titles available from
WORDS DANCE PUBLISHING

a poem by kris ryan

Unrequited love? We've all been there.

Enter:

WHAT TO DO AFTER SHE SAYS NO
by Kris Ryan.

This skillfully designed 10-part poem explores what it's like to ache for someone. This is the book you buy yourself or a friend when you are going through a breakup or a one-sided crush, it's the perfect balance between aha, humor & heartbreak.

WHAT TO DO AFTER SHE SAYS NO
A Poem by Kris Ryan

$10 | 104 pages | 5" x 8" | softcover | ISBN: 978-0615870045

"*What to Do After She Says No* takes us from Shanghai to the interior of a refrigerator, but mostly dwells inside the injured human heart, exploring the aftermath of emotional betrayal. This poem is a compact blast of brutality, with such instructions as "Climb onto the roof and jump off. If you break your leg, you are awake. If you land without injury, pinch and twist at your arm until you wake up." Ryan's use of the imperative often leads us to a reality where pain is the only outcome, but this piece is not without tenderness, and certainly not without play, with sounds and images ricocheting off each other throughout. Anticipate the poetry you wish you knew about during your last bad breakup; this poem offers a first "foothold to climb out" from that universal experience."

— LISA MANGINI

"Reading Kris Ryan's *What To Do After She Says No* is like watching your heart pound outside of your chest. Both an unsettling visual experience and a hurricane of sadness and rebirth—this book demands more than just your attention, it takes a little bit of your soul, and in the end, makes everything feel whole again."

— JOHN DORSEY
author of **Tombstone Factory**

"*What to Do After She Says No* is exquisite. Truly, perfectly exquisite. It pulls you in on a familiar and wild ride of a heart blown open and a mind twisting in an effort to figure it all out. It's raw and vibrant...and in the same breath comforting. I want to crawl inside this book and live in a world where heartache is expressed so magnificently.

— JO ANNA ROTHMAN
MA, Coach & Conjurer of Electric Creative Wholeness

Other titles available from
WORDS DANCE PUBLISHING

Tammy Foster Brewer is the type of poet who makes me wish I could write poetry instead of novels. From motherhood to love to work, Tammy's poems highlight the extraordinary in the ordinary and leave the reader wondering how he did not notice what was underneath all along. I first heard Tammy read 'The Problem is with Semantics' months ago, and it's stayed with me ever since. Now that I've read the entire collection, I only hope I can make room to keep every one of her poems in my heart and mind tomorrow and beyond.

— **NICOLE ROSS**, author

NO GLASS ALLOWED
Poetry by Tammy Foster Brewer

$12 | 56 pages | 6" x 9" | softcover | ISBN: 978-0615870007

Brewer's collection is filled with uncanny details that readers will wear like the accessories of womanhood. Fishing the Chattahoochee, sideways trees, pollen on a car, white dresses and breast milk, and so much more -- all parts of a deeply intellectual pondering of what is often painful and human regarding the other halves of mothers and daughters, husbands and wives, lovers and lost lovers, children and parents.

— **NICHOLAS BELARDES**
author of *Songs of the Glue Machines*

Tammy deftly juxtaposes distinct imagery with stories that seem to collide in her brilliant poetic mind. Stories of transmissions and trees and the words we utter, or don't. Of floods and forgiveness, conversations and car lanes, bread and beginnings, awe and expectations, desire and leaps of faith that leave one breathless, and renewed.

"When I say I am a poet / I mean my house has many windows" has to be one of the best descriptions of what it's like to be a contemporary female poet who not only holds down a day job and raises a family, but whose mind and heart regularly file away fleeting images and ideas that might later be woven into something permanent, and perhaps even beautiful. This ability is not easily acquired. It takes effort, and time, and the type of determination only some writers, like Tammy, possess and are willing to actively exercise.

— **KAREN DEGROOT CARTER**
author of *One Sister's Song*

DO YOU WRITE POETRY?
Submit it to our biweekly online magazine!

We publish poems every Tuesday & Thursday on website.

Come see what all the fuss is about!

We like Poems that sneak up on you. Poems that make out with you. Poems that bloody your mouth just to kiss it clean. Poems that bite your cheek so you spend all day tonguing the wound. Poems that vandalize your heart. Poems that act like a tin can phone connecting you to your childhood. Fire Alarm Poems. Glitterbomb Poems. Jailbreak Poems. Poems that could marry the land or the sea; that are both the hero & the villain. Poems that are the matches when there is a city-wide power outage. Poems that throw you overboard just dive in & save your ass. Poems that push you down on the stoop in front of history's door screaming at you to knock. Poems that are soft enough to fall asleep on. Poems that will still be clinging to the walls inside of your bones on your 90th birthday. We like poems. Submit yours.

WORDSDANCE.COM

WORDS DANCE
PUBLISHING